Storied Sips

Storied Sips

Evocative cocktails for everyday escapes, with 40 recipes

ERICA DUECY

collages by POUL LANGE

Random House Reference
New York Toronto London Sydney Auckland

Collages, drink photography, and calligraphy: copyright © 2013 by Poul Lange

Credits: Amanda D'Acierno, *senior VP, publisher*; Fabrizio La Rocca, *VP, creative director*; Tina Malaney, *associate art director*; Chie Ushio, *senior designer*; Jennifer Romains, *manager*; Erica Duecy and Kayoko Suzuki-Lange, *photo styling*; Amy Metsch, *VP, associate publisher*; Maren Monitello, *editor*; Sue Daulton, *VP, operations*; Tom Marshall, *associate director, production*; Alison Skrabek, *associate director, managing editorial*; Kaitlyn Robinson, *managing editor*; Ciara Robinson, *production editor*; Katie Fleming, *senior publicist*

Visit the Random House Web site: www.randomhouse.com

ISBN: 978-0-375-42621-6

Printed in China

10 9 8 7 6 5 4 3 2 1

First Edition

To Jono & Gia

Contents

stir with cracked ice, strain.

Introduction

Take a trip in a sip, a journey through time and place in this spirited collection of cocktails. Spanning some 200 years, from Europe to the Far East, cocktail history is brimming over with intriguing stories. The libations in *Storied Sips* are the ones with the best tales to tell, from the Mojito's pirate legacy to the Margarita's Old Hollywood ties.

These cocktails are more than just drinks. They have helped define eras, reinforce social customs, fête the seasons, and mark historic events. Some cocktails have even become icons, conveying messages about personal style, social status, and cultural trends in their conical glasses.

In our everyday lives, cocktails can inspire wanderlust, encourage romance, and lubricate social situations, among their many applications. The drinks may be refreshing or warming, calming or invigorating. And they add an undeniably festive edge to any event—revelers sipping brilliantly colored concoctions, ice cubes tinkling as the background track, and the bartender shaking up another round. On an even more quotidian level, cocktails can also provide a delicious little daily escape, an elegant reward for a hard day's work.

✳ ✳ ✳ ✳ ✳

In the early days, cocktails weren't indulgences, but rather curative remedies. The first-known definition of the word appeared in the May 13, 1806 issue of *The Balance and Columbia Repository* in Hudson, New York. The paper's editor wrote: "Cock tail, then is a stimulating liquor, composed of spirits of any kind, sugar, water and bitters..."

Bitters were the key to the cocktail's healing powers. Used since the eighteenth century in England, these high-proof tonics infused with botanicals, herbs, and barks were said to cure stomach ailments, headaches, indigestion, or other maladies (see the Pimm's Cup, p. 82). By the mid-1800s, there were hundreds of bitters brands in the United States, including Peychaud's from New Orleans (crucial to the Sazerac cocktail, p. 174) and Angostura, made by a German doctor in Venezuela. The overblown curative powers of bitters — some claimed to cure malaria or other serious diseases — led to bitters being disparaged as "snake oils".

But whether or not one believed in the medical efficacy of sipping bitters with spirits, there was no denying that they made most liquor taste better. The consumption of healing bitters also added an air of legitimacy to drinking establishments where patrons would show up in the morning for an eye-opener (the best is the Corpse Reviver No. 2, p. 98), and then again for a midmorning bracer, lunchtime fortifier, afternoon reviver, evening aperitif, and finally, the necessary nightcap.

European cultures have been mixing spirits and liqueurs with wines and juices for generations, with aperitifs like the Kir Royal (p. 34) and Portonic (p. 30) as evidence. But cocktails are a uniquely American innovation. During the Golden Age of mixology in the late nineteenth and early twentieth centuries, all parts of the country were involved in the creation of new drinks that have become classics. The Mint Julep (p. 146) showcased bourbon, Kentucky's proudest export. The Sazerac highlighted New Orleans' homegrown Peychaud's bitters. The Manhattan (p. 178) reflected New York City sophistication.

Meanwhile, as American bartenders and drinks enthusiasts fanned out around the world, they took their thirst for cocktails along, inspiring new drink creations, from the Hemingway Daiquiri (p. 86) in Cuba to the Pisco Sour (p. 74) in Peru. Further afield, colonial outposts in the Far East even contributed a few notable classics, including the house cocktail at Burma's Pegu Club (p. 130) and the Singapore Sling (p. 154) from the landmark Raffles Hotel in Singapore.

During Prohibition, from 1920 to 1934, most bitters brands died off, and cocktail culture suffered a major blow. Cocktails were still being invented, but mostly outside of the United States (with the exception of Detroit's memorable Last Word, p. 110). Europe was a major center for innovation during that dry period, with cocktails like the Sidecar (p. 126) and Royal Highball (p. 46) emerging from across the pond.

After World War II, cocktail culture began its resurgence. Drinks that were already considered classics, like the Manhattan and the Martini, made a comeback. More than any others, those cocktails typified mid-century modern life, the era of the office Martini cart and the three-Martini lunch.

With a growing middle class in the late 1940s, travel to tropical places was an exotic new reality. Whether boarding planes to places like French Polynesia, Puerto Rico, and Mexico, or just armchair travelling, a new thirst for tropical experiences propelled drinks like the Mai Tai (p. 162), Piña Colada (p. 106), and Margarita (p. 102) into the mainstream.

By the time the Cosmopolitan (p. 122) emerged in the late 1980s, cocktail culture had hit a low point. Most cocktails

resembled convenience store slushies—brightly colored, sugary drinks served in supersize quantities.

The turn of the millennium marked the beginning of a cocktail renaissance. In just about any city in the country, you can find bars using fresh juices, and some that even make their own bitters and vermouths.

Even better, home bartenders have gotten in on the act, learning the classics, refining their techniques, and adding their own tweaks to this infinitely adaptable art form. Cocktail parties are no longer the domain of cheap vodka and canned juices, but rather an outlet for sophisticated cocktails served in vintage glassware with top-shelf ingredients.

With the bar raised to new heights, there's no better time to take a journey through cocktail history. We'll celebrate the craft's most notable stories, toast the ingenuity of drink innovators, and sip our way through the best cocktails of the past 200 years. Cheers!

Bar Essentials

The process of making a cocktail is an aesthetic treat in itself. There's the pleasurable anticipation, pondering what you'll make. The selection of exquisite glassware, shiny bottles, and exotic liqueurs. A few moments of precise measuring and mixing, and voilà! A well-made cocktail is a thing of beauty, worthy of contemplation as it passes your lips.

Quality over quantity is the philosophy that will elevate your cocktails to the heights of Jazz Age glamour. Spirits and liqueurs should be top-shelf (or at least a cut above standard), juices freshly squeezed, and glasses shined to a sparkling finish. Herewith are the tools and techniques to help you make the most memorable cocktails.

Classic Glassware

There's nothing more disheartening than drinking the last few lukewarm sips of a Martini. Save yourself the disappointment by making cocktails in smaller glasses, which can be found in vintage shops and specialty retailers online. Most cocktails in this book are around four ounces for short drinks without ice, and around eight ounces for long drinks served over ice. Each recipe in this book specifies a glass shown here.

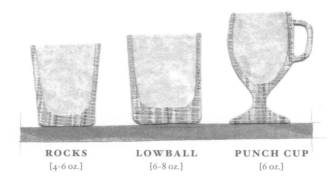

ROCKS
[4-6 oz.]

LOWBALL
[6-8 oz.]

PUNCH CUP
[6 oz.]

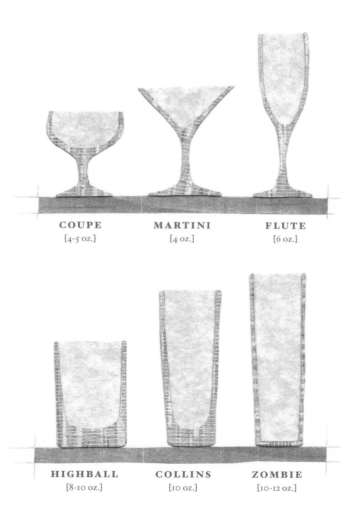

COUPE
[4-5 oz.]

MARTINI
[4 oz.]

FLUTE
[6 oz.]

HIGHBALL
[8-10 oz.]

COLLINS
[10 oz.]

ZOMBIE
[10-12 oz.]

Quality Ingredients

A good cocktail requires fresh ingredients, from juices squeezed that day to recently opened vermouths (keep vermouth for up to three months in the refrigerator). In certain recipes, spirit and liqueur brands are mentioned where they make a significant difference to the resulting cocktail. These are a few must-have ingredients for your home bar.

Amarena cherries—instead of the nuclear red-colored variety, try this darker, more complex Italian type of preserved cherries for an elegant garnish.

Bitters—these high-proof mixtures of botanicals, herbs, and spices add layers of complexity to a cocktail. Angostura and Peychaud's are essential. Also look for orange bitters and other varieties—even celery and chocolate flavors—from producers like Fee Brothers and The Bitter Truth.

Fresh juice—simply put, there is no excuse for using canned or bottled juices in a cocktail. Once you've had a cocktail made with fresh juices, you'll never go back to the shelf-stabilized stuff.

Grenadine—this pomegranate syrup is an essential sweet-tart ingredient in many classic recipes. Most commercially produced grenadines taste awful. To make your own, heat one cup of unsweetened, 100% pomegranate juice and ¾ cup sugar over medium heat, stirring regularly, until the sugar melts and the solution's cloudiness dissipates. (For even more flavor com-

plexity, add a tablespoon of pomegranate molasses to the hot syrup.) Cool, keep in refrigerator for up to one month, and use as needed.

Ice—spherical ice or square cubes make a lovely presentation in the glass. Silicone molds in a variety of sizes are easily found online.

Simple syrup—in a small saucepan, warm one cup of sugar and one cup of water over medium heat, stirring regularly, until the sugar melts and the solution's cloudiness dissipates. Cool, keep in refrigerator, and use as needed.

Tonic—instead of the typical yellow-label stuff, try a small-batch version for more flavor and less sugar, like Q Tonic or Fever Tree.

Top-shelf liquors—splurge on a few bottles to easily elevate the quality of your cocktails. You'll find specific brands mentioned in the book where they make a notable difference.

Vermouth — I think it's fair to say that many cocktail enthusiasts have never even tasted vermouth on its own—even a tiny sip. A good vermouth is *really* good. Alone. Over ice. With a bit of soda and a citrus twist. By definition, vermouth is just fortified wine with herbs and botanicals. Until recently, most have come from Europe. For classic cocktails, I typically recommend the following: For dry vermouth (a.k.a. white, French), try Noilly Prat and Dolin Vermouth de Chambéry. For sweet vermouth (a.k.a. red, Italian), I like Cinzano and Carpano Antica Formula.

Back in the States, there's something of an American vermouth renaissance afoot. In recent years, small, artisanal brands like Atsby, Vya, and Uncouth Vermouth have emerged, with their assertive styles and fascinating flavors. These vermouths focus on local sourcing and innovative ingredient combinations (think shiitake mushrooms, lavender, caramel, and celery). They're great for sipping, or for adding new flair to classic cocktail recipes.

Proper Tools

There are a few essential tools you'll need for your home bar. Many liquor stores and kitchen stores carry these products, as do online retailers.

Citrus peeler—you need a sharp implement to easily peel pith-free strips off a lemon or lime, for flavor or garnish. Use a citrus peeler for thin strips, a vegetable peeler for wide strips.

Jiggers—these double-sided measuring cups come in a variety of sizes. Most useful are the half-ounce and one ounce cups, and the one-and-a-half and two ounce versions.

Juice squeezer—handheld squeezers are useful for small quantities of citrus, but prevent a cramped hand and use a tabletop squeezer when a big batch is required.

Metal shaker—cobbler shakers are most common for home bartenders, with mixing tin, strainer lid, and cap.

Mixing glass—these beautiful, oversize crystal glasses with a spout are ideal for making a mixed drink that doesn't require shaking. Or substitute a large, wide-bottomed glass.

Muddler—this blunt-ended tool is used to mash fruit and sugar at the bottom of a cup, essential for some recipes. In a pinch, use the handle of a wooden spoon.

Strainer—to keep ice and fruit bits out of your drink, use a metal strainer that allows only liquid to pass from the shaker into the glass.

Cocktails

Bellini

Harry's Bar is situated in Venice on an unassuming corner just off of the Grand Canal, close to St. Mark's Square. From the outside, you'd never guess that this nondescript watering hole was once a clubhouse to famous American expats and travelers in Italy, from Charlie Chaplin and Ernest Hemingway to Barbara Hutton and Peggy Guggenheim. But enter through the frosted glass doors and, even today, the refined midcentury ambiance is palpable with its white-tuxedoed barmen and elegantly suited maître d' who graciously welcomes guests as if they were regulars.

Giuseppe Cipriani, the founder of Harry's Bar, created the Bellini sometime in the 1930s, based on a traditional Italian

PEACH

recipe of marinating peaches in white wine to make a sangria-like drink. But Cipriani wanted to make a more elegant version for his celebrity clientele, so he pureed white peaches and added them to festive Prosecco, a Northern Italian sparkling wine, yielding an attractive pink cocktail that would become world famous. After an exhibition of paintings by Renaissance artist Giovanni Bellini came through Venice in 1948, Cipriani christened the cocktail the Bellini, for the painter's use of a particular shade of pink in several of his works that matched the color of the cocktail. Whether served at brunch or aperitivo, the Bellini adds a celebratory glow to any gathering.

BELLINI

2 ounces white peach puree

4 ounces Prosecco (Italian sparkling wine), chilled

Glass: flute

To a chilled flute, add white peach puree. Fill remainder of glass with Prosecco.

MIMOSA
Popularized as a brunch drink at the Ritz Hotel in Paris in the 1920s, the Mimosa is made from two ounces orange juice and 4 ounces Champagne, served in a flute.

Portonic

Imagine arriving for your wine tasting at a *quinta* estate on steeply terraced vineyards overlooking the Douro Valley, in Portugal. You've driven here on winding roads with the sun beating down on your shoulders, and now you're ready for a drink. But the rich port wines you've come to taste just aren't going to cut it. Or are they? On a silver tray headed your way are tall glasses filled with a sparkling, golden elixir. The Portonic is grown-up lemonade, a thirst-quenching blend of white port and tonic water that is gently bitter-sweet with floral and honey notes.

This classic Portuguese aperitif stars the little-known style of port wine made from white grapes instead of red, which are

then fortified with grape brandy. Most people think of port as a ruby red after-dinner tipple, but not this stuff. With fresh, vibrant flavors, white port is better suited to festive brunches and hazy wine-tasting afternoons. Make the Portonic by the glass, or better yet, by the pitcher. The aperitif is so low in alcohol that you can indulge in a round (or three) before dinner and still be the life of the party.

PORTONIC

2 ounces white port

4 ounces good tonic, such as Q Tonic or Fever Tree

Dash Angostura bitters

Glass: collins

Garnish: lemon wedge and mint sprig

Fill a collins glass with ice. Add all ingredients to glass and stir gently. Garnish with lemon wedge and mint sprig.

Kir Royal

There's nothing more French than sitting at a sidewalk café in a Burgundian village, sipping a Kir Royal at sunset. The simple, yet elegant fusion of sparkling wine with crème de cassis, a blackcurrant liqueur, makes a festive start to an evening as townspeople wander by and the sun sets lazily over the vineyards of the Cote d'Or. For generations, locals have been drinking the sparkling and non-sparkling version of the drink as an evening aperitif, but it was a Catholic priest turned German resistance fighter who elevated the drink to the world stage. Today the everyday version, called a Kir, uses tart, white aligoté wine, while the sparkling version uses Champagne or Crémant de Borgogne.

Canon Felix Kir worked for decades as a clergyman before the German occupation of Dijon during World War II, when he became a vocal opponent to Nazi Germany and helped thousands of French prisoners escape from a detainee camp.

At the war's conclusion, Kir was elected mayor of Dijon and became a vocal advocate for local products, including Burgundy's wines and liqueurs. Kir served his namesake drink to visiting dignitaries and at official functions, making it the region's signature aperitif. Today, the white wine version is a classic everyday quaff from Paris to Marseilles, while the sparkling version kicks off evening celebrations around the world.

KIR ROYAL

½ ounce crème de cassis

5 ounces Brut Champagne

Glass: flute

Garnish: lemon twist

Add crème de cassis to a chilled flute.
Top glass with Champagne. Garnish with
a lemon twist.

KIR

For an everyday aperitif, pour ½ ounce of
crème de cassis into a wine glass and top with
about 5 ounces of a dry, un-oaked white wine,
such as aligoté or Pinot Grigio.

Aperol Spritz

Throughout Rome, in bustling squares like Campo de Fiori each evening, you'll find outdoor café tables filled with locals gathered for *aperitivo*. The treasured nightly ritual is a time to unwind with a cocktail, preferably a Spritz, a deep orange sparkler featuring Prosecco and Aperol, the bittersweet citrus liqueur that has been quenching the thirst of Italians since 1919. Aperol debuted that year at the Padua International Fair, created by brothers Luigi and Silvio Barbieri of the Barbieri Company, a liqueur manufacturer. Revolutionary for its time was Aperol's low alcohol content of 11%, about half as much as Campari. Early advertisements call the aperitivo "il liquore degli sportive," or "the liquor for active people," for its low alcohol content.

— 8 —

S'i' son curvo un po' di dietro,
Molto bene sto dinanzi:
E la serva del Cananzi
Mel ripete tutto dì.

APEROL

SERENATA LIVORNESE.

Via Fontona,

Like most other bitter liqueurs, Aperol's ingredients are a tightly held secret. A few of the known components in the thirty-ingredient elixir include medicinally active plants like gentian (anti-inflammatory) and cinchona bark (from which quinine is derived), as well as aromatic herbs and plants like rhubarb, mandarin orange peel, and bitter orange peel. Regardless of its supposed health benefits, Aperol and its namesake Spritz have taken off in popularity in recent decades, becoming the signature drink of Italy. You won't find the Spritz on most menus, but that speaks to the cocktail's ubiquity: Locals know they can order it anywhere.

APEROL SPRITZ

4-6 ounces Prosecco or other sparkling wine

1 ½ ounces Aperol

Splash of club soda

Slice of orange

Glass: highball or balloon wine glass

Fill a highball with ice. Pour in Prosecco
and Aperol and top with club soda. Stir.
Squeeze the orange slice into the cocktail,
and submerge it.

Bamboo Cocktail

In 1859, Yokohama's port opened to international trade, ushering in Japan's modern era. Soon, European and American dignitaries, merchants, and traders were streaming forth from grand steamships to explore the country and its opportunities. For those who could afford it, the Grand Hotel, opened in 1873, was *the* place to stay. The hotel was considered the best Western-style lodging in Japan during its reign (it was destroyed in a 1923 earthquake), advertising such luxuries as a French chef, extensive wine list, and a steam launch that would meet guests at their incoming ships to expedite their luggage through customs.

THE GRAND HOTEL, YOKOHAMA, JAPAN.

PROMISES TO PAY THE BEARER
AND ONE YEN IN GOLD.

A German barman turned hotel manager, Louis Eppinger, took over the reigns at Grand Hotel in 1891 and is credited with creating the Bamboo Cocktail shortly thereafter.

Other than its name and point of origin, there's really nothing that ties this cocktail to Japan. Made from sherry and dry vermouth with two types of bitters, it is a smooth, low-alcohol sipper, ideal for an afternoon aperitif. The 1908 *World's Drinks and How to Mix Them*, by William Boothby, calls for the Bamboo with equal parts sherry and vermouth, but experts in Japan claim that recipe is incorrect. Order the cocktail today at the New Grand Hotel in Yokohama, built after the original burned, and you'll receive a drink with three parts sherry to one part vermouth.

BAMBOO COCKTAIL

2 ounces sherry (fino for a lighter version; dry amontillado for a richer cocktail)

2 ounces Dolin dry vermouth

2 dashes orange bitters

Dash Angostura bitters

Glass: coupe

Garnish: lemon twist

Fill a coupe with ice to chill. In a mixing glass filled with ice, add all of the ingredients and stir thoroughly. Empty ice from coupe and strain cocktail into it. Garnish with lemon twist.

本
證
明
書
ハ
他
人
ニ
貸
與
シ
又
ハ
讓
渡
ス
ヘ
カ

THE GRAND HOTEL, YOKOHAMA, JAPAN.

Royal Highball

Since 1898, The Ritz Hotel in Paris has played host to celebrities and royals, from Coco Chanel and Marcel Proust to Cole Porter and F. Scott Fitzgerald. The hotel's bar has specialized in catering to the whims of a demanding clientele, including King Alfonso XII of Spain, who was a regular in the 1920s. Legend has it that the Royal Highball cocktail was developed by renowned Ritz barman Frank Meier in honor of King Alfonso at the opening of the Ritz bar, in 1921. The festive, yet strong sparkler is made from Cognac, Champagne, and muddled strawberries.

In acknowledgement of King Alfonso's seemingly limitless appetite of Champagne and spirits, Meier would serve the

cocktail in a large highball glass, nearly double the size of a typical Champagne flute. But, apparently, the king grew increasingly dedicated to his "more is more" motto over the years. Georges Scheuer, a manager at the Ritz bar for forty years, reminisced decades later that King Alfonso "was automatically served his special drink, a quart of Dom Pérignon Champagne liberally laced with Cognac, and a dozen strawberries," upon entering the bar. Bemused regulars took to ordering the drink by an alternate name when His Highness was not present. They winkingly called it "King's Death."

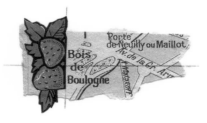

ROYAL HIGHBALL

4 ripe strawberries

1 ounce Cognac, such as Hennessy

4 to 6 ounces Champagne

Glass: highball or flute

Muddle strawberries in the bottom of a
mixing glass, then strain strawberry juice into
a flute. Add Cognac and Champagne to flute;
stir lightly.

Tom Collins

In the early 1880s, the Tom Collins hoax swept New York, inspiring copycat pranks, tribute songs—and even a cocktail. Several newspapers, including this account from 1874, described the hoax similarly:

> "'A joker meets a friend and accosts him with 'Have you seen Tom Collins?' 'No, who the deuce is Tom Collins?' 'Well, I don't know much about him, but he says he knows all about you and is telling terrible lies and scandals...'"

The joker then tells the victim to look for Tom Collins at the saloon around the corner, but in that bar and every other one he enters, he is told that Tom Collins has just left. The victim eventually realizes he has been tricked, and the hoaxer buys him drinks.

OLD TOM
possesses a very fragrant and agreeable odor and
taste, characteristic of Gin of good quality,"—
Tom Collins
A
Humorous Song
BY
FRANK WILDER.

The game so captured the minds of New Yorkers that it spawned several songs like "Tom Collins is My Name," with its lyrics "I'm here, I'm there, I'm everywhere / And rather hard to find / So don't attempt to look me up / Unless you're well inclined."

In 1876, "Professor" Jerry Thomas published the first-known recipe for the Tom Collins, a cocktail featuring "old Tom gin," a sweetened version of gin that was popular in the nineteenth century. Mixed in a tall, ice-filled glass with lemon juice, sugar, and soda water, the Tom Collins is a gin-spiked sparkling lemonade perfect for hot summer afternoons.

TOM COLLINS

1 teaspoon superfine sugar (omit if using Old Tom gin)

½ ounce lemon juice

2 ounces London dry gin or Old Tom gin, like Hayman's

6 to 8 ounces soda water

Glass: collins

Garnish: lemon peel

To a collins glass, add sugar and lemon juice. Mix to dissolve sugar, then add gin, several ice cubes, and soda water. Mix gently to combine. Submerge a long strip of lemon peel into the glass so it spirals around the ice cubes.

OLD TOM GIN.

The flavor is particularly pleasant, due to the Juniper and other aromatic ingredients which have been used. Altogether this Gin may be said to be of very superior quality."

Elderflower Gin Fizz

In the foothills of the French Alps each spring, foragers hike into the forests with canvas sacks slung over their shoulders, in search of elderflowers. These prized white blossoms of the elder shrub—with their ephemeral lychee-pear scent—bloom for just a few weeks a year. The flowers are hand-harvested, then transformed overnight by local artisans into teas and cordials, before the delicate blossoms lose their intoxicating scent. Some elderflowers are also rushed to a distillery, where they become that year's batch of St-Germain elderflower liqueur.

These days, St-Germain is used in myriad cocktails, but one of the most notable is an updated rendition of a Gin Fizz, a

GIN

ST·GERMAIN

classic that is nearly forgotten. Back in the early 1950s, the Gin Fizz was Paris' most fashionable cocktail. Lubin perfumer Henri Giboulet was so captivated by the drink and another notable American export—film star Grace Kelly—that he created a perfume called Gin Fizz, said to capture the *joie de vivre* and chic American elegance they both represented. With its honeyed sweetness and floral notes, St-Germain adds a delicious dimension to the Gin Fizz, of which Giboulet would surely approve.

ELDERFLOWER GIN FIZZ

2 ounces gin

1 ounce St-Germain

1 ounce lemon juice

1 teaspoon superfine sugar

Club soda

Glass: highball

In an ice-filled shaker, add all ingredients except the soda. Shake for about 15 seconds. Strain into an ice-filled highball glass and top with soda.

INGÉNUE COCKTAIL
For an elegant aperitif, mix 5 ounces Champagne with 1 ounce St-Germain and serve in a flute.

Adhésifs résistant

INDEX ALPHABÉTIQUE

Vocabulaire du livre relié.

Crocodile : cuir......

ELECTRIC CLOUD WITH LIGHTNING ON SIDE OF ANDES.

Moscow Mule

It's hard to recall a time when vodka wasn't America's most popular spirit. But the clear, odorless firewater wasn't commonly available in the United States until the late 1940s, and even then lagged behind gin, rum, and whiskey for decades. Vodka's first breakout cocktail hit? It was not the Martini, but rather the Moscow Mule, a spicy refresher made from vodka, ginger beer, and lime juice, served in a copper mug. The cocktail—which became popular in Hollywood, then tentacled out around the country—wasn't created by a clever bartender, but by the owner of Smirnoff, signifying the first time a cocktail was created as a marketing device.

It was 1946 when John Martin, the American owner of the Smirnoff brand, reconnected with Jack Morgan, his friend who owned the Cock'n Bull, a bar on the Sunset Strip in Los Angeles. That year, *LIFE* magazine called the Cock'n Bull one of the country's five most famous drinking establishments, due to its popularity with movie stars. At the time, Smirnoff wasn't selling well, and neither was Cock'n Bull-branded ginger beer. A third friend also had a suffering copper manufacturing business. Necessity being the mother of invention, the trio developed the idea of the Moscow Mule—complete with its copper mug—and the concept took off, becoming vodka's most popular cocktail until it was surpassed by the vodka Martini in the 1970s.

MOSCOW MULE

2 ounces vodka

½ ounce lime juice

6 ounces ginger beer

Glass: lowball or copper mug

Garnish: lime wedge

Fill lowball glass with ice. Add vodka, lime juice, and ginger beer; stir. Garnish with a lime wedge.

French 75

One of the few classic cocktails to emerge during Prohibition, the French 75 cocktail is named after a fast-firing, seventy-five-millimeter field artillery used in World War I. The nimble weapon was crucial to helping to procure victory for the Allied Troops and American Expeditionary Forces. Much like the weapon, the cocktail "hits with remarkable precision," wrote Harry Craddock in his 1930 *Savoy Cocktail Book*. The simple elixir of gin, sugar, lemon juice, and Champagne is surprisingly potent (if you swapped out the Champagne for soda water, you'd get a Tom Collins—but that's another story).

75 Although the French 75's precise origin is disputed (there are competing claims from French, British, and American bars), the cocktail was popularized stateside at the Stork Club, a posh Manhattan nightclub that was the apex of Manhattan's café culture in the 1930s. Tallulah Bankhead, Jack Benny, Doris Duke, and Orson Welles were among the celebrity clientele that frequented the venue, rubbing shoulders with royals and politicians as they sipped the day's most fashionable cocktail. The tart, refreshing sparkler is just as relevant and appealing today as it was at the height of the Jazz Age. But don't be surprised by its howitzer-like kick after a round or two.

FRENCH 75

1 ounce London dry gin

¾ ounce lemon juice

½ ounce simple syrup

4 ounces Brut Champagne

Glass: flute

Combine all ingredients except Champagne
in a cocktail shaker and shake vigorously.
Strain into a chilled flute, and fill remainder
of glass with Champagne.

Mamie Taylor

In 1899, ladies' day dresses were high-collared, corseted affairs, with long, full skirts. Not the best sailing attire, especially for a famed singer with a penchant for drama. Perhaps Mayme Taylor, the *prima donna* of an opera company performing in Rochester, New York, had overdressed for the occasion. In any case, she returned from a sailing outing on Lake Ontario one hot summer day and collapsed on a hotel lawn chair, requesting a popular refresher at the time, claret lemonade (red wine mixed with lemonade). Lacking those ingredients, the barman whipped up what looked to be a tall glass of Champagne, on ice.

But what crossed Taylor's lips was far more intriguing. Subtly smoky, citrusy, and gingery, the cocktail was like nothing Taylor had tried before. After allowing her entourage to sample the mystery concoction, they declared it utterly refreshing. Taylor summoned the barman to ask what the drink was called. "A Mayme Taylor," he replied, without hesitation. The combination of scotch, ginger beer, and lime juice quickly caught on. In 1902, the *Syracuse Post-Standard* recounted the story, noting that the cocktail "seemed to meet with instantaneous favour [sic] and has become famous all over the country." The notoriety of the Mamie Taylor cocktail (the spelling inexplicably evolved) seems to have boosted the singer's career. Before long, she was performing in Manhattan, on Broadway's biggest stages.

MAMIE TAYLOR

½ ounce lime juice

2 ounces blended Scotch

4 to 6 ounces ginger beer

Glass: highball

Garnish: lime wedge

Fill highball glass with ice. Squeeze half a lime
into the glass, then add Scotch. Top with
ginger beer, and garnish with a lime wedge.

Mojito

The Mojito is said to date back to the late 16th century, when the Caribbean seas were terrorized by pirates and privateers robbing ships of Peruvian gold and other New World riches *en route* to Europe. Sir Francis Drake, knighted by Britain's Queen Elizabeth I, was one of the most successful privateers working for the British crown. The Spaniards called him El Draque (The Dragon) for his successful attacks on Spain-bound ships. Legend has it that one of Drake's subordinates honored him with a Mojito-esque drink called El Draque, made from the ingredients they carried on board: *aguardiente de cana* (an early form of rum), mixed with lime juice, sugar, and Cuban mint.

HAVANA

H

CUBA

SCALE OF MILES
0   20   40   60   80

SCALE OF KILOMETRES
0   20   40   60   80

Sloppy Joe's Ron Drinks

MOJITO

1 Teaspoonful of sugar.
One half a lime.
1 Part of Rum.
Seltzer water.
Leaves of Mint.
Shell of lime.
Serve in a High Ball glass with
Cracked ice.

SLOPPY JOE'S
RON SUPERIOR
Sloppy Joe's Bar

HABANA CUBA

PRODUCT OF CUBA
AGED IN WOOD DISTILLED

Sloppy Joe's Bar
HAVANA   CUBA

Four centuries later, the drink was re-popularized as the Mojito during Prohibition in Havana, with much the same recipe.

At the time, Havana was the nightclub capital of the world, and just a forty-minute flight from Miami. Travelers would disembark into a tropical oasis of rum and rumba, Cohibas and cabaret. The most famous Mojito bar in Havana was (and is) La Bodeguita del Medio, a dive-bar whose A-list clientele in those early years included Nat King Cole, Ernest Hemingway, and Errol Flynn. There, they drank Mojitos alongside local fans of the cocktail, such as Che Guevara and a young Fidel Castro. Some recipes call for a tame white rum, but for a revolution-worthy Mojito, be sure to use a deeply flavored, aged, premium rum.

MOJITO

2 teaspoons superfine sugar

6 mint leaves

2 ounces aged rum

¾ ounce lime juice

Soda water

Glass: highball

Garnish: lime wedge

Add sugar and mint leaves to a highball glass and muddle to crush the leaves. Fill with ice. Add rum and lime juice; stir. Fill remainder of glass with soda water. Garnish with lime wedge.

My mojito in La Bodeguita
My daiquiri in El Floridita

Ernest Hemingway

Pisco Sour

Of all the rivalries that exist between Chile and Peru—best soccer team, coolest capital city—the birthplace of the Pisco Sour may be the most hotly contested. Both countries claim ownership of the frothy citrus cocktail. Although not wise to mention in front of a *chileno*, most drinks historians now credit the drink to Victor Vaughn Morris, a bartender from Salt Lake City who moved to Lima, Peru, and opened a bar there in 1916. Morris' bar became popular among international travelers for its Pisco Sour, a local variation on a whiskey sour, a common drink of that era.

Pisco is a brandy made in Chile and Peru from local grapes, but the products are not interchangeable: Chilean pisco tends to be a little sweeter, with a slightly lower proof.

Although the Pisco Sour started out as a simple sour, it evolved into a superior cocktail when a bartender at Morris' bar added egg white to give it a silky texture and frothy head. That innovation made the Pisco Sour into a sophisticated lemon meringue pie-like drink—but without any cloying sweetness. Pisco's earthy notes and Angostura's complex spice prevent the cocktail from becoming a dessert staple. Instead, the tart, light Pisco Sour makes an impressive opener for any Latin-themed party.

PISCO SOUR

2 ½ ounces Chilean Pisco

¾ ounce fresh lemon or lime juice

1 egg white (or 2 tablespoons pasteurized, liquid egg whites)

½ ounce simple syrup

4 dashes Angostura bitters

Glass: coupe

Fill a coupe with ice to chill. In an ice-filled shaker, add all of the ingredients except bitters and shake for about 15 seconds. Empty ice from coupe and strain cocktail into it. Dash bitters on top of froth.

Aviation

Airplanes were still called "aeroplanes" around the time the Aviation cocktail was created in the early 1900s. The pioneering field of flight was hot—the Wright Brothers were national heroes and passenger flight was in its infancy. It was no surprise that a cocktail celebrated these exciting innovations. But for decades, people wondered why a clear drink with gin, maraschino liqueur, and lemon juice was called an Aviation. That three-ingredient recipe appeared in the *Savoy Cocktail Book*, a 1930 bar manual by Harry Craddock, a famous American barman who worked at the Savoy Hotel in London during Prohibition. Most people assumed he was the drink's creator.

Then, in 2004, cocktail historian David Wondrich stumbled upon a beat-up booklet by New York barman Hugo R. Ensslin called *Recipes for Mixed Drinks*, and made an exciting discovery. The earlier, 1916 recipe collection—now recognized as the last American cocktail book published before Prohibition—features the Aviation with one significant change: the addition of crème de violette, a floral, purple liqueur. A few drops of this elixir yields an elegant, more complex version of the Aviation that is—notably—colored a brilliant sky blue. With that addition, the name suddenly became self-explanatory.

AVIATION

2 ounces London dry gin

¾ ounce lemon juice

¼ ounce maraschino liqueur

¼ ounce crème de violette

Glass: coupe

Fill a coupe with ice to chill. In a shaker filled with ice, add all of the ingredients and shake until frost forms on the shaker. Empty ice from martini glass and strain cocktail into the glass.

THE STRATOSPHERE
For an alluring aperitif, mix Champagne with a few dashes of crème de violette, as they did at New York's rollicking Stork Club, a favorite celebrity haunt of the mid-twentieth century.

Pimm's Cup

The Wimbledon Tennis Championships. British Polo Day. The Henley Royal Regatta. England's poshest sporting events have something unexpected in common: a signature cocktail, the Pimm's Cup. The sparkly refresher is made from Pimm's No. 1, a gin-based tonic, along with carbonated lemonade or ginger beer, and an extensive garnish that can wander into fruit salad territory. The Pimm's Cup legacy goes back to 1840s London, when James Pimm, a London oyster bar owner, developed the formula as a digestion aid. Infused with spices and liqueurs, the Pimm's Cup was so tasty that it soon surpassed a popular drink at the time, the gin sling—made from gin, sugar, and water. Before long, the Pimm's Cup was appear-

PIMM'S

THE ORIGINAL Nº1 CUP

ing instead of gin slings at picnics and garden parties across the English countryside.

The Pimm's brand was so successful in those early days that it branched out into other versions to reflect the tastes of the times. The earliest variation in the 1850s was Pimm's No. 2 Cup, a Scotch-based formula, while the vodka-based Pimm's No. 6 was developed a century later in the 1960s. The original Pimm's No. 1 gin-based version still remains the most popular formula—though its exact ingredients are a closely held secret. But one needn't travel across the pond for a taste of Britain's uppercrust indulgences; just buy a bottle of Pimm's No. 1, and pull out the croquet set. Then—pinky extended—enjoy a Pimm's Cup while whacking balls out on the lawn. As they say in the U.K., it's always "Pimm's o'clock."

PIMM'S CUP

2 ounces Pimm's No. 1

4 ounces ginger beer or sparkling lemonade

Glass: collins

Garnish: cucumber slice, sprig fresh mint
(5 to 6 leaves)

Fill a collins glass with ice. Add Pimm's
and ginger beer or sparkling lemonade, and
stir well. Garnish with cucumber slice
and mint sprig.

Hemingway Daiquiri

The origin of the Daiquiri has always been hotly debated. Cocktail chronicler Charles H. Baker Jr. devoted a page of his 1939 *Gentleman's Companion, Vol. II*, to debunking several competing claims before positing his own theory, which so far has never been disproved. According to Baker, the Daiquiri was created in Cuba in 1898. In the months following the Spanish-American War, a group of American engineers were dispatched to oversee operations at an iron mine in the village of Daiquiri, near Santiago de Cuba. Using the ingredients they had on hand—rum, lime, and sugar—they created a drink that was destined to become a classic.

The Daiquiri soon became a hit with locals and visitors. Ernest Hemingway regularly sipped them at El Floridita Bar in Havana in the 1930s and 1940s, and helped expand the Daiquiri's repertoire by requesting a tasty variation that caught on. The addition of maraschino liqueur and grapefruit juice to a Daiquiri came to be known as a Hemingway Daiquiri, or Papa Doble (Hemingway ordered doubles). Although it clashes with his manly image, Hemingway preferred his Daiquiris blended. But they were a far cry from the frozen confections served at many bars today. Hemingway famously distained sugar in his cocktails, so his self-styled Daiquiris were always tart and strong—even if they did look like pink slushies.

HEMINGWAY DAIQUIRI

2 ounces golden rum

¾ ounce fresh lime juice

½ ounce maraschino liqueur

1 ounce pink grapefruit juice

Glass: coupe

Garnish: amarena cherry

In a blender filled with half a cup of crushed ice, add all of the ingredients and blend until smooth. Pour cocktail into a coupe glass. Garnish with amarena cherry.

ORIGINAL DAIQUIRI
In a lowball glass, add a teaspoon of superfine sugar and the juice of half a lime. Mix with a spoon until sugar dissolves. Add spent lime shell to glass, then add several large ice cubes and 2 ounces golden rum.

El Diablo

Tequila is a relatively recent addition to the bartender's palette. While gin and whiskey starred in cocktails as far back as the eighteenth century, tequila was a novelty until Prohibition, when many Americans headed south of the border to slake their thirst. As Mexico became an easy, tropical getaway for the flourishing middle class in the late 1940s, the Margarita—and the infamous tequila shot—became a mainstay at pool parties around Southern California, and then at backyard barbecues around the country. But after the Margarita's great leap forward, creativity with the agave spirit largely stalled—except in one unexpected corner.

Victor "Trader Vic" Bergeron, the California-based founder of Trader Vic's restaurants, and father of tiki culture, was a

EL DIABLO

EL MÚSICO

LA ESCALERA

rum devotee. But even Bergeron got caught up in the tequila craze long enough to create one memorable cocktail. In his 1946 *Trader Vic's Book of Food and Drink*, Bergeron lists the first-known recipe for El Diablo (a.k.a. The Devil). Made from tequila, crème de cassis, lime juice, and ginger beer, the drink is a mildly spicy, citrus and berry refresher that allows the pleasing herbal and vegetal notes of the tequila to come through. It may have taken seventy years, but El Diablo is finally hitting its peak, appearing on cocktail menus around the country. It will most certainly become known as a modern classic.

EL DIABLO

Juice from half a lime

1 ½ ounces tequila

½ ounce crème de cassis

4 to 6 ounces ginger beer

Glass: highball

Squeeze lime juice into a highball glass and drop shell of lime into it. Add ice, tequila, and crème de cassis. Fill rest of glass with ginger beer, and stir gently.

EL CATRIN   LA DAMA

Jack Rose

The Jack Rose is a cocktail with colonial—and even presidential—history. When Scotsman William Laird settled in New Jersey in 1698, the distiller applied his craft to the most abundant natural resource in the area, apples, to make a whiskey-like spirit called applejack, an oak-aged apple brandy mixed with grain alcohol. The product was a hit with early colonists, who didn't drink much water for fear of disease. Instead, they sipped spirits like applejack as morning pick-me-ups, lunchtime bracers, afternoon fortifiers, post-meal digestifs, and pre-bed nightcaps. George Washington even got in on the action, making the Laird family recipe at his distillery in Virginia.

By the early 1900s, bartenders were mixing up Jack Rose cocktails, with applejack, lemon or lime juice, and grenadine, a tart-sweet pomegranate syrup. A tabloid called *The National Police Gazette* contains the first-known reference to the cocktail, attributing it in a 1905 squib to "Frank J. May, better known as Jack Rose," who tended bar at Gene Sullivan's Cafe on Pavonia Avenue in Jersey City. Then again, the cocktail is so deeply colored that it's "the exact shade of a Jacqueminot rose" (abbreviated as Jack Rose), according to the 1934 *Old Waldorf-Astoria Bar Book*. Whatever the true origin of its name, there's no denying the festive cheer a Jack Rose cocktail can bring to any evening.

JACK ROSE

2 ounces applejack

¾ ounce lemon juice

¾ ounce grenadine

Glass: coupe

Fill coupe with ice water to chill. In an ice-filled shaker, add all of the ingredients and shake for about 15 seconds. Empty ice from coupe and strain cocktail into it.

PAN AMERICAN CLIPPER
Charles Baker's 1939 *Gentleman's Companion* features this more complex version of a Jack Rose. To an ice-filled shaker, add 1½ ounces applejack, ¾ ounce lime juice, ¼ ounce grenadine, and 1 dash absinthe. Strain into a chilled coupe.

Corpse Reviver No. 2

The glamorous American Bar at the Savoy Hotel in London has been one of the world's most influential cocktail destinations since it opened in 1889. During Prohibition, the Art Deco lounge was home to talented American bartenders like Harry Craddock, author of the 1930 *Savoy Cocktail Book,* who shook up cocktails for the likes of Ava Gardner, Charlie Chaplin, and Errol Flynn. Back in those days, restorative morning "eye openers" were part of a drink enthusiast's repertoire. Also called "corpse revivers", these were prescriptive drinks meant "to be taken before 11 A.M., or whenever steam and energy are needed," Craddock notes.

2

The early twentieth century saw many such breakfast drinks, used to remedy hangovers and to steel oneself for the day ahead. Most of these formulations are forgettable, but one stands out for its timeless appeal. The Corpse Reviver No. 2 first appeared in Craddock's book and is a complex, elegant gin-based cocktail, featuring the aromatic wine-based Lillet, orange Cointreau liqueur, lemon juice, and a dash of absinthe. In fact, it's so tasty that a word of caution may be warranted. As Craddock wisely remarks, "Four of these taken in swift succession will unrevive the corpse again."

CORPSE REVIVER NO. 2

1 ounce London dry gin

1 ounce Lillet Blanc

1 ounce Cointreau

1 ounce lemon juice

Dash absinthe

Glass: coupe

Fill a coupe with ice to chill. In an ice-filled shaker, add all of the ingredients and shake for about 15 seconds. Empty ice from coupe and strain cocktail into it.

Dull morning look...

Snap back with dazzle!

Margarita

During Prohibition, Mexico was the closest place to Hollywood to get a legal cocktail. Droves of American movie stars and socialites vacationed south of the border, bringing drinks like the Daisy—a basic formula involving a spirit, in concert with lemon juice and a liquid sweetener—along with them to their hotels and holiday villas. From there, some clever (or thirsty) person made a Daisy with tequila. The Spanish name for daisy? Margarita. The drink became a hit among the Hollywood set, but not before dozens of would-be inventors—from star-struck bartenders to Texas socialites—stepped forward to claim it as their own.

One of the most compelling stories involves a gorgeous sixteen-year-old dancer named Margarita Cansino. Too young to work in Los Angeles, she was regularly escorted by her dance-instructor father to perform at the Agua Caliente Hotel, an elegant gaming resort in Tijuana that was popular with celebrities like Clark Gable, Jean Harlow, and Charlie Chaplin. A bartender there was so enamored with Cansino that he created a special cocktail and named it after her. Like the cocktail, the dancer was also discovered at the Agua Caliente and went on to achieve international fame. Margarita Cansino's stage name? Rita Hayworth.

MARGARITA

2 ounces tequila

1 ounce Cointreau

1 ounce lime juice

Glass: martini

Garnish: coarse salt

Roll the wet rim of a martini glass in coarse
salt. In an ice-filled shaker, add all ingredients
and shake for about 15 seconds.
Strain into salt-rimmed martini glass.

Piña Colada

With the 1949 opening of the Caribe Hilton Hotel, Puerto Rico became a jet-set playground. As the first major tourist development on the island, the hotel was quickly inundated with Hollywood stars and international travelers. The modern, white high-rise on a private peninsula in San Juan is still one of the city's most stunning properties, with its white-sand beach, lush gardens, and endless ocean views.

It was there, in 1954, that Ramon "Monchito" Marrero, a bartender at the Beachcomber Bar, was given an assignment: Create a cocktail that captures the flavors of Puerto Rico in a glass. For months, Marrero experimented, finally hitting his epiphany.

Using light rum, freshly pressed pineapple juice, and Coco Lopez coconut cream, a new product that had recently been developed on the island, Marrero blended together the ingredients and called the result a "piña colada," Spanish for "strained pineapple." The original recipe blended up into a delicate, creamy cloud that was cool, strong, and not too sweet—a perfect poolside companion. Soon, Marrero was serving the drink to notable guests like John Wayne, Gloria Swanson, and Elizabeth Taylor. The frosty cocktail is now served at beach bars around the world, but is still most closely aligned with Puerto Rico, where it has been the country's official drink since 1978.

PIÑA COLADA

2 ounces rum (use light rum for a milder cocktail, dark for more richness and complexity)

1 ounce coconut cream

3 ounces fresh pineapple juice

Glass: lowball

Garnish: pineapple slice and amarena cherry, speared on toothpick

Add rum, cream of coconut, pineapple juice, and a cup of crushed ice to a blender. Frappe for 15 seconds and pour into a lowball glass. Garnish with pineapple slice and amarena cherry.

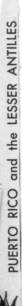

PUERTO RICO and the LESSER ANTILLES

Last Word

At the Detroit Athletic Club, doormen have been greet-
ing guests in top hats and coattails since 1915. Clubhouse to
Olympic athletes, automotive titans, and Midwestern politicians during Detroit's heyday, the DAC was (and is) the city's
most elite gathering place. It is also home to the Last Word,
a remarkable Prohibition-era cocktail. During that thirsty
time, Detroit was a major thoroughfare for bootleggers, so
the DAC elite didn't have to go far for a cocktail. In their
ball gowns and tuxedos, members snuck out the club's back
door to the "DAC Annex" speakeasy, conveniently located
behind it.

How the club's—or, ahem—speakeasy's bartenders procured the Last Word's relatively exotic ingredients is anyone's guess. But thankfully, someone whipped up the aromatic, limey elixir. Gin and lime juice, common bar partners, meet two unlikely glass-mates in Chartreuse, a bitter, herbal spirit from France, and Luxardo Maraschino, a bittersweet cherry liqueur from Italy. Lean in for a sip and you're enveloped in a delicious cloud of cherries and herbs.

Sadly, the cocktail languished in obscurity for decades after it was published in Ted Saucier's 1951 bar book, *Bottoms Up*. But recently, dedicated cocktailians have resurrected the Last Word. To try one at the source, though, you may have to twist the arm of a well-heeled Detroiter: The DAC is still members' only. Or you could try that back door.

LAST WORD

1 ounce London dry gin

1 ounce Luxardo Maraschino

1 ounce Chartreuse liqueur

1 ounce lime juice

Glass: martini

Garnish: amarena cherry, submerged

Fill a martini glass with ice to chill. In an ice-filled shaker, add all of the ingredients and shake for about 15 seconds. Empty ice from glass and strain cocktail into it. Garnish with amarena cherry.

Death in the Afternoon

It's hard to guess what Ernest Hemingway loved more: women and weapons, or booze and boats. That latter combination was channeled by the hard-charging writer in *So Red the Nose, or Breath in the Afternoon*, a 1935 celebrity cocktail book to which Hemingway contributed one of his own creations. Of the cocktail's origin, Hemingway writes, "This was arrived at by the author and three officers of *H. M. S. Danae* after having spent seven hours overboard trying to get Capt. Bra Saunders' fishing boat off a bank where she had gone with us in a N. W. gale." Apparently, a strong cocktail with a celebratory air was required after the trying nautical mishap.

Absinthe and Champagne, two of Hemingway's favorite libations, fit the bill nicely. In fact, they're the only two ingredients in this spirited drink, which is as precise and potent as Hemingway's prose. Hemingway named the cocktail Death in the Afternoon, referencing his book about bullfighting in Spain. Perhaps the name pays homage to Spain itself, where Hemingway continued drinking absinthe long after it was banned in France and the United States. Or he may be referring to the likely effect of the cocktail if sipped as prescribed. As Hemingway questionably instructs readers: "Drink three to five of these slowly."

DEATH IN THE AFTERNOON

1 ½ ounces absinthe

4 ounces brut Champagne, chilled

Glass: flute

Pour absinthe into a chilled flute. Add
Champagne slowly as the drink takes on a
milky appearance.

Martini

More than any other cocktail, the Martini is imbued with lore, intrigue, and symbolism. It has played a central role in pop culture for more than a century, and is the only cocktail to have its own visual signifier—the sleek, conical Martini glass. Order a Martini, and suddenly you're swept into the Las Vegas Sands of the 1960s, with Dean Martin, Frank Sinatra, and Sammy Davis Jr. performing onstage, riffing off one another midway through their "Drunk Singers" number in tuxedoes, with a big band accompaniment. Or maybe *your* Martini takes you to the hallowed chambers of Manhattan's Four Seasons restaurant, closing a deal with fellow midcentury power brokers over a three-Martini lunch.

The history of the Martini goes back even further, to around the 1880s, with numerous schools of thought as to its origin.

The West Coast hypothesis finds the Gold Rush in full swing, with the Martinez cocktail (a relatively close precursor) created in the Bay Area for a gold-mining clientele. The East Coast hypothesis finds the Martini being served at New York's swanky Hoffman House hotel, or at another bar around town.

Martini devotees—like followers of most faiths—tend to have strong opinions about their rules of practice. Whether gin or vodka, wet or dry, lemon twist or olive garnished, the variations of Martini worship are seemingly limitless.

MARTINI

3 ounces London dry gin or vodka

¼ ounce dry vermouth

Glass: martini

Garnish: lemon twist or pimento-stuffed Spanish olive

Fill martini glass with ice to chill. In an ice-filled mixing glass, add both ingredients. Stir for about 15 seconds. Empty ice from glass and strain cocktail into it. Garnish as desired.

MARTINEZ

"Professor" Jerry Thomas' 1887 bar guide, from his time working at San Francisco's Occidental Hotel, gives a recipe that's more like a reverse, sweet Martini. The recipe calls for 1 ounce Old Tom gin, 2 ounces sweet (red) vermouth, 2 dashes Maraschino liqueur, and 1 dash orange bitters.

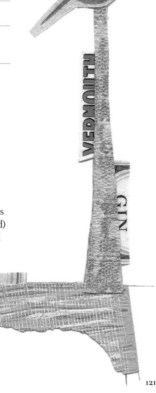

Cosmopolitan

The Cosmopolitan is the Elizabeth Taylor of cocktails, with her tangled history, gaudy-yet-glamorous appeal, and public highs and lows. The Cosmopolitan's origin story zigzags the country, with paternity claims from San Francisco to New York City. One plausible story from Miami's South Beach finds bartender Cheryl Cook testing a new product, Absolut Citron, in the late 1980s at The Strand. She tweaks the Kamikaze by substituting Absolut Citron, adds cranberry juice to make it look "oh so pretty in pink," and boom—the Cosmopolitan is born. Soon, the Cosmo appears on drink menus from coast to coast.

By the mid-1990s, Dale DeGroff adds the Cosmopolitan to his menu at New York's Rainbow Room, upgrading it with Cointreau and fresh lime juice. Around that time, the Cosmopolitan becomes Carrie Bradshaw's signature tipple on *Sex and the City*, and the cocktail is catapulted into stratospheric, worldwide popularity, where it remains for much of the following decade. Then, like Ms. Taylor and countless stars before her, the Cosmopolitan suffers a period of eye-rolling overexposure that requires her to take a break from the public eye.

These days, the cocktail occasionally is cast in small, indie roles as the Pomegranate Cosmo or the Ginger Cosmo. But someday, the original tart-sweet Cosmopolitan will come back, in all her glory, to endure as a modern classic. It's just a matter of time.

COSMOPOLITAN

1 ½ ounces citrus vodka

¾ ounce cranberry juice

½ ounce Cointreau

½ ounce fresh lime juice

Glass: martini

Garnish: lemon twist

Fill a martini glass with ice to chill. In an ice-filled shaker, add all of the ingredients and shake for about 15 seconds. Empty ice from glass and strain cocktail into it. Garnish with the lemon twist.

Sidecar

For homesick American and British expatriates, Harry's New York Bar in Paris has provided a taste of home since its 1911 opening. Writers like F. Scott Fitzgerald, Sinclair Lewis, and Ian Fleming frequented Harry's Bar during their stays in the city for its inventive cocktails and masculine ambiance. American college pennants and British university shields adorn the bar's dark, mahogany-paneled walls, providing a dramatic backdrop for a cocktail that has become a classic. The saloon's bartender (and later owner), Scotsman Harry MacElhone was responsible for creating several well-known drinks and popularizing the Sidecar, a drink he based on the earlier Brandy Crusta.

The Sidecar is a simplified Brandy Crusta which was created in the 1850s by restaurant manager Joseph Santini at New Orleans' City Exchange. The Brandy Crusta—so named for the sugar crust on the rim of the glass—was innovative for its time, marking the first-known instance citrus juice was used in a cocktail. Streamlining and upgrading the Crusta—using premium Cognac, Cointreau, and lemon juice—was MacElhone's contribution, making the tart, powerful Sidecar. To try the cocktail at the source, Harry's Bar famously instructs patrons to tell their taxi driver, "Sank Roo Doe Noo." That should get you to the bar, at 5 rue Daunou.

SIDECAR

1 ½ ounces Cognac, such as Hennessy

1 ounce Cointreau

1 ounce lemon juice

Glass: coupe

Garnish: superfine sugar

Dip wet rim of a coupe in superfine sugar. In an ice-filled shaker, add all ingredients and shake for 15 seconds. Strain into coupe with sugared rim.

BRANDY CRUSTA
Mix 1 ½ ounces brandy, 1 ½ ounce Cointreau, ¾ ounce lemon juice, ¼ ounce maraschino liqueur, and 1 dash Angostura bitters. Shake over ice and strain into a sugar-rimmed coupe. Submerge a large, wide strip of lemon peel.

Pegu Club

The Pegu Club was a British outpost of gin and gentility in Burma, from the late 1880s through World War II. Located just outside of Rangoon, the officer's club was so fabled that Edward VIII, Prince of Wales, ate dinner there on his tour of Southeast Asia's British colonies in 1921. A Reuters reporter who accompanied the prince recounted that day in Rangoon. Following a parade to honor his arrival, the prince played in a polo match with Burmese jockeys "in terrifically colored jackets and caps," then retired to the Pegu Club for dinner. "The dinner at the Pegu Club and the dance which followed it ... will form long-lived memories in Rangoon," the reporter said.

W&K
LONDON.   H.R.H. THE PRINCE OF WALES.   No 152

A Burmese Woman

Pegu Club — Rangoon

Like other well-known colonial clubs of its day, the Pegu Club had a signature drink. But unlike many others, this cocktail is worth remembering—and drinking. The appeal of the Pegu Club is its Martini-like sophistication, with just a dash of tropical flavor. Starting with a base of gin, and building in orange liqueur, lime juice, and bitters, served up, the drink—like the club—offered a taste of home with a twist. By 1930, the cocktail had attained legendary status. That year, the *Savoy Cocktail Book* noted that the Pegu Club cocktail was "one that has traveled, and is asked for, around the world."

PEGU CLUB

1 ½ ounces gin

½ ounce Cointreau

½ ounce lime juice

Dash orange bitters

Dash Angostura bitters

Glass: coupe

Fill a coupe with ice to chill. In an ice-filled shaker, add all of the ingredients and shake for about 15 seconds. Empty ice from coupe and strain cocktail into it.

Negroni

Even in the early 1900s, Florence was a famous center of arts and culture. In those days, horse-drawn carriages ferried Florentine aristocrats and international dignitaries to Gothic marvels like the famed Duomo and the Uffizi Gallery, home to a priceless collection of Renaissance art. On the tony Via Tornabuoni, alongside high fashion boutiques, Caffè Casoni was the center of Florentine society, frequented by well-heeled locals and foreigners. There, the dapper barman Fosco Scarselli held court, preparing cocktails and espressos with a side of society gossip.

One of the most popular cocktails Scarselli served was the Milano-Torino, a drink made from equal parts of the bit-

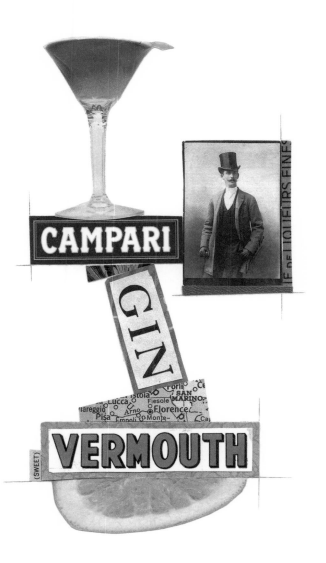

ter orange Campari liqueur (from Milan) and the herbal Cinzano red vermouth (from Torino), along with a splash of soda water. The cocktail is now called the Americano, for the early twentieth-century American tourists who ordered them with abandon.

As legend has it, one day Count Camillio Negroni, who was a regular customer at the Casoni, asked Scarselli to make his Milano-Torino "a bit stronger," perhaps with gin. The gallivanting nobleman had recently returned from London, where he had grown fond of the botanical-infused spirit. Soon, customers from near and far were asking for gin Americanos, or "Negroni's drink," and a classic was born.

NEGRONI

1 ounce London dry gin

1 ounce Campari

1 ounce sweet vermouth

Glass: martini

Garnish: orange twist

Fill a martini glass with ice to chill. In an ice-filled shaker, add all of the ingredients and shake for about 15 seconds. Empty ice from glass and strain cocktail into it. Garnish with orange twist.

AMERICANO
To make a lighter cocktail with the bitter-sweet complexity of a Negroni, mix equal parts Campari and red vermouth in a collins glass filled with ice, then top with soda water. Garnish with orange twist.

Bitter CAMPARI

Ti stampo col cor.

Sul tuo seno

Vieni, o bella,

Ed un bacio d'amor

Napoléon's Opera

Around the time of Napoléon Bonaparte's final defeat in Belgium, in 1815, the French emperor heard a strange tale. At a nearby abbey in Biercée, a chemist was said to be making a mandarin-scented spirit. Bonaparte, who hailed from the orange-growing island of Corsica, questioned the tale — no citrus fruits grew this far north — yet he was intrigued. He visited the abbey distillery and, indeed, there was a distillate being made from dried mandarin orange peels. Bonaparte was so enamored with this reminder of his childhood home that he asked the chemist to blend the orange essence with Cognac from his personal collection.

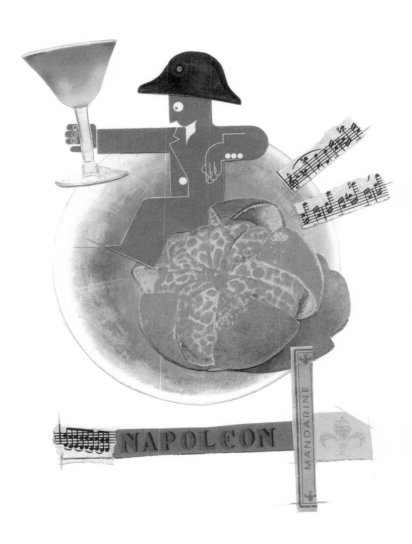

That off-the-cuff blending session—and others that followed—inspired Mandarine Napoléon, a liqueur that combines mandarin distillate, ten-year-old Cognac, and spices like green tea, cardamom, cinnamon, and nutmeg. Years later, in 1892, the chemist's family released the product to honor Bonaparte's memory.

In this modern cocktail, Mandarine Napoléon is mixed with gin and a French favorite—the aperitif wine Dubonnet Rouge—in a spirited tribute to another one of Bonaparte's most noted passions: the opera.

NAPOLÉON'S OPERA

1 ½ ounces London dry gin

¾ ounce Mandarine Napoléon

½ ounce Dubonnet Rouge

3 dashes Angostura bitters

Glass: coupe

Fill a coupe with ice to chill. In an ice-filled shaker, add all of the ingredients and shake for about 15 seconds. Empty ice from coupe and strain cocktail into it. Garnish with an orange twist.

Source: Adapted from Jim Meehan, PDT (Please Don't Tell), New York, New York

Stork Club Cocktail

Beginning in 1930, until it closed in 1965, everyone who was anyone went to the Stork Club. The New York nightclub and restaurant was a hangout for the country's elite, from entertainers like Frank Sinatra and Lucille Ball to politicians like Ronald Regan and John F. Kennedy. On any given night, the "King of Swing" Benny Goodman and his orchestra would be performing, while the club's patrons canoodled over Champagne, cocktails, and caviar. Society writer Lucius Beebe summed up the club's status in a 1946 book: "To millions and millions of people all over the world the Stork symbolizes and epitomizes the *de luxe* upholstery of quintessentially urban existence. It means fame; it means wealth; it means an elegant way of life among celebrated folk."

Along with a desirable social scene, the Stork Club was known for its world-class cocktail program. Chief barman Nathaniel "Cookie" Cook and his crew invented dozens of drinks, including the club's signature libation, the Stork Club Cocktail. Featuring sweetened Old Tom gin, along with freshly squeezed orange and lime juice, Cointreau, and bitters, the drink is pleasantly tangy and endlessly quaffable. The tangerine-hued cocktail added a splash of color to the club's dark-paneled formal dining room, sipped by executives in their tuxedoes and debutantes and fashion models in their strapless gowns. At this temple to café society, the Stork Club Cocktail was the *most* stylish glass to raise.

STORK CLUB COCKTAIL

1 ½ ounces Hayman's Old Tom gin

1 ounce freshly squeezed orange juice

¼ ounce lime juice

¼ ounce Cointreau

Dash Angostura bitters

Glass: coupe

Garnish: orange twist

Fill a coupe with ice to chill. To an
ice-filled shaker, add all ingredients and
shake for about 15 seconds. Empty coupe
and strain cocktail into it. Garnish with
orange twist.

Mint Julep

Fashionable ladies in wide-brimmed hats. Starry-eyed gamblers placing bets. Horses twitching as they approach the gates. And ... they're off! The annual Kentucky Derby is horse-racing's biggest event, and the state's day to shine on the world stage. So it's no surprise that Kentucky's most famous export—bourbon—rides front and center. Since the first running of the Derby, in 1875, the festivities have been celebrated with Mint Juleps. The sweet, minty mound of bourbon-soaked snow is a refreshing, yet potent cocktail. It can take the edge off a betting loss, or contribute to the celebration of a lucky trifecta winner.

Distillers have been making whiskey in Kentucky since the first European settlements there. The simple cocktail of bourbon, sugar, and mint, is a highly ritualized process that has inspired endless tributes.

Kentucky newspaper man J. Soule Smith wrote an "Ode to the Mint Julep" in the 1890s: "When it is made, sip it slowly. August suns are shining, the breath of the southern wind is upon you. It is fragrant, cold and sweet—it is seductive. No maiden's kiss is tenderer or more refreshing; no maiden's touch could be more passionate. Sip it and dream—you cannot dream amiss."

MINT JULEP

6 mint leaves

1 teaspoon sugar

3 ounces bourbon

6 mint leaves

Glass: lowball or silver julep cup

Garnish: mint sprig

In lowball or julep cup, add 6 mint leaves and sugar; crush with muddler. Fill glass with finely crushed ice. Pour bourbon over ice and stir. Garnish with mint sprig.

Planter's Punch

Planter's Punch is a Jamaican creation so delicious that it inspires poetry—at least that's what historic recipes would have you believe. The cocktail has appeared in rhyming verse in dozens of publications, including the earliest known reference, a 1878 squib in the London magazine *Fun*: "A wine-glass with lemon juice fill / Of sugar the same glass fill twice / Then rub them together until / The mixture looks smooth, soft, and nice. / Of rum then three wine glasses add / And four of cold water please take. A drink then you'll have that's not bad / At least, so they say in Jamaica."

In simple terms, the classic recipe breaks down as one sour (lemon, lime); two sweet (grenadine, sugar); three strong

PLANTER'S PUNCH

JAMAICA

RUM RUM RUM

Montego Bay
S. Negril Pt.
Savanna la Mar
Black River
Falmouth
St. Ann's Bay
Port Maria
Annotto Bay
Port Antonio
Blue Mountain Pk.
7,388
Ewarton
Spanish Town
Portland
Point
Kingston
Morant Point
JAMAICA
(Br.)
Pedro Bank

WORLD FAMOUS
DARK AND MELLOW

(rum); and four weak (water, fruit juice). With wildly varying ingredients and proportions from those early specifications, Planter's Punch is more of a class of cocktails, though some recipes are certainly better than others. Globetrotting cocktail writer Charles Baker included no fewer than ten Planter's Punch recipes in his 1939 book, *The Gentleman's Companion, Vol. II*, advising his readers to use "decent well-aged" rums in these punches. He concludes, "Just because they are a bit disguised with tropical fruit juice is no sign that thirty seconds swizzling, shaking, or stirring will make up for the eight years the raw spirit should have lain in wood casks." Start with the recipe here, then improvise at will.

PLANTER'S PUNCH

2 ounces dark rum

1 ounce lime juice

1 ounce pineapple juice

½ ounce simple syrup

2 dashes Angostura bitters

Glass: collins

Garnish: grated nutmeg and lime wedge

In an ice-filled shaker, add all ingredients and shake for 15 seconds. Strain mixture into an ice-filled collins glass. Stir well to combine. Grate nutmeg over top and garnish with lime wedge.

JAMAICA RUM

Pedro Bank

Pedro Cays
(Jamaica)

Morant Cays
(Jamaica)

Singapore Sling

In the early 1900s, Raffles Hotel Singapore was the *de facto* clubhouse of European diplomats, adventurers, and writers visiting Singapore, a British Crown Colony at the time. At midday, women with parasols, high-collared blouses, and long skirts poured out of rickshaws in the sweltering streets, stepping into the fan-cooled embrace of the hotel. Leisurely lunches were enjoyed on the shaded verandah, accompanied by cooling drinks—but little booze. Ladies did not commonly order alcoholic drinks in public at the time, so the hotel's Chinese bartender Ngiam Tong Boon often served fruit juice.

Occasionally, Mr. Ngiam would get a sly request to spike the drink. These appeals prompted him to innovate on a common refresher— the gin sling. The drink of sweetened gin and water over ice, sometimes with liqueurs added for color and flavor, was already popular in turn-of-the-century Singapore. Mr. Ngiam is said to have innovated by adding pineapple juice to mask the alcohol and grenadine to give a pretty pink color. The cocktail was an immediate hit with Mr. Ngiam's female clientele and became famous worldwide. Sadly, the original recipe has been lost to time, though the Raffles Hotel Singapore still serves the most recognized version, recorded on a bar receipt from 1936. A drier version is presented here for sophisticated sippers who still want a taste of Singapore's history.

SINGAPORE SLING

1 ounce London dry gin

1 ounce Cherry Heering

1 ounce grenadine

1 ounce pineapple juice

1 ounce fresh lime juice

1 ounce soda water

1 dash Angostura bitters

Glass: zombie

Garnish: pineapple wedge

Add first five ingredients to a shaker filled
with ice. Shake for about 15 seconds.
Strain into an ice-filled zombie glass. Add
soda water and bitters. Garnish with a
pineapple wedge.

Singapore. Raffles Hotel.

Dark & Stormy

In 1806, James Gosling boarded the British ship *Mercury*, bound for Virginia. His father, a London liquor shop owner, had chartered the vessel and filled it with European wines and spirits to be sold in the newly independent United States. But Gosling never made it to America. The boat charter expired before reaching the states, and the captain dumped the young man and his cargo at the nearest British-controlled port: St. Georges, Bermuda. Unexpectedly, Gosling took a liking to the subtropical island and decided to stay, opening a liquor shop on Front Street.

From that unlikely start, the Gosling family built a Bermudian rum empire, first importing distillates from around the West

GINGER

BEER

RUM

Indies in the 1860s and blending them in Bermuda. Customers called smoky, molasses-tinged rum "black seal," for the dark wax that sealed the rum bottles.

By the early 1900s, locals were mixing Gosling's Black Seal rum with another island product, ginger beer, to make the Dark & Stormy cocktail. The spicy, sweet drink—trademarked by Gosling's—is as synonymous with the island as pink beaches, sun-baked yachties, and knee-length shorts. Look for authentic Dark & Stormy cocktails (the dark rum should roil like an angry sky into light ginger beer) at port-side bars along the Eastern seaboard, and beyond.

DARK & STORMY

4 ounces ginger beer

¼ ounce fresh lime juice

2 ounces Gosling's Black Seal rum

Glass: collins

Garnish: lime wedge

In an ice-filled collins glass, add the ginger beer and lime juice. Slowly pour rum into the glass, so a layer forms between the ginger beer and rum. Garnish with lime wedge.

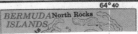

Mai Tai

At the end of World War II in 1945, soldiers brought home stories and souvenirs from the exotic South Pacific. Flower leis, grass skirts, flaming torches, and mysterious totems swept into America's collective imagination, generating a flood of Polynesian-themed restaurants and bars. Trader Vic's, a restaurant in Oakland, California, was an early entrant owned by Victor (Trader Vic) Bergeron. Bergeron's restaurant was a few years old by the time he started work on his opus, a cocktail that would be his contribution to the tiki pantheon. "I thought about all the really successful drinks: Martinis, Manhattans, Daquiris ... all basically simple drinks," he observed, and started mixing.

RUM

TRADER VIC'S

MAI TAI

Bergeron's intention was to create a high-quality classic that didn't need to be weighed down with the dozen or so ingredients in most tiki drinks. The idea was to let the spirit shine. "I took down a bottle of seventeen-year-old rum," he described, adding to it fresh lime juice, along with small amounts of orange liqueur, orgeat syrup, and sugar syrup.

The drink quickly became famous. It was drier and more complex than many of the rum punches Bergeron had made before, thus appealing to a wider base of imbibers. As for the name? Friends from Tahiti were at the restaurant when he mixed up an early round. After a sip, they agreed, "mai tai — roa ae," which in Tahitian means "out of this world."

MAI TAI

2 ounces aged dark rum

½ ounce orgeat (almond) syrup

½ ounce Cointreau

¼ ounce simple syrup

Juice from 1 fresh lime

Glass: lowball

Garnish: lime shell and mint sprig

Add all liquid ingredients, plus the shell from half a lime, to shaker. Shake vigorously for about 15 seconds, and pour contents into an ice-filled lowball glass. Fill glass with ice and garnish with a mint sprig.

Old Fashioned

The Old Fashioned cocktail has been old–fashioned since at least the 1880s. The first-known definition of a cocktail, in a New York newspaper in 1806, defines it as "a stimulating liquor, composed of spirits of any kind, sugar, water and bitters." Make that stimulating liquor a rye or bourbon whiskey, and you're looking at the basic recipe for an Old Fashioned cocktail.

The earliest printed reference to an Old Fashioned comes from the *Chicago Tribune* in 1880. When Samuel J. Tilden, who had been defeated in the U.S. presidential race of 1876 under questionable circumstances, announced that he would not run again, his opponents raised their glasses: "Hot whiskies... sour mashes, and old-fashioned cocktails were drank in honor of the event."

By the following decade, in 1890, the *New York Sun* newspaper described the Old Fashioned cocktail as "very soothing and grateful to the palate," also noting that "this latest drink of the habitues of Madison Square is a return to Pike County simplicity." Comprising a bitters-soaked sugar cube, ice, and whiskey, along with a garnish, the formula seems perfectly straightforward. But dozens of minute variations exist, from the type of whiskey to the inclusion of soda water. Some enthusiasts swear by a muddled "garnish" of a cherry and orange slice, while others scoff at this "fruit salad" approach, preferring instead a lemon twist. Whatever your preference, savor the taste of American history next time you take a sip.

OLD FASHIONED

3 dashes Angostura bitters

1 sugar cube

2 ounces bourbon or rye whiskey

Glass: rocks

Garnish: lemon twist

In a rocks glass, dash bitters onto sugar cube;
crush with a muddler. Add one large ice cube,
then pour in whiskey and stir. Garnish with
lemon twist.

Blood & Sand

Like its namesake film, the appeal of this cocktail rides on the sensual interplay of masculine and feminine elements. The 1922 silent movie *Blood and Sand* made a star of Rudolph Valentino, designating him as one of film's first sex symbols. The Great Lover, as he was called, was known for his elegant beauty. An obituary after his untimely death at age 31 remarks: "Always he was a favorite with women, from girls in grammar school to elderly ladies, but the one taunt he could not stand was that he was a ladies' man, an effeminate." His outlet for those charges was to take on masculine roles, like the bullfighter he played in *Blood and Sand*.

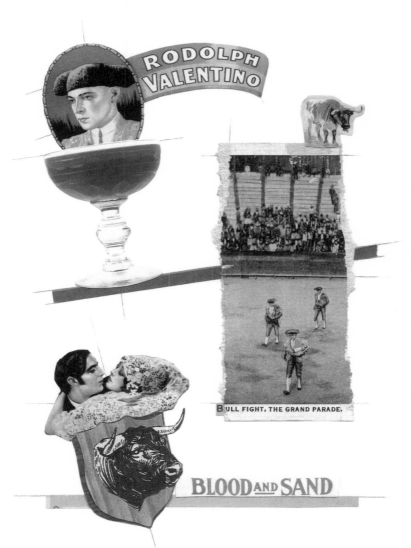

RODOLPH VALENTINO

BULL FIGHT, THE GRAND PARADE.

BLOOD AND SAND

The Blood & Sand cocktail, which first appears in the 1930 *Savoy Cocktail Book*, channels Valentino's spirit with its masculine-feminine appeal.

Scotch, the spirit of old boys' clubs, comprises the backbone of this drink. With its assertive, smoky character, Scotch has rarely been employed in a memorable cocktail. But here, this sand-colored spirit shines in an unlikely meeting with the "blood" ingredients of the cocktail equation, a delicate, fruity cherry brandy and sweet vermouth. The resulting drink is more than the sum of its parts, a smoldering, luscious cocktail that seduces on the first sip.

BLOOD & SAND

1 ounce blended Scotch whisky,
such as Famous Grouse

1 ounce orange juice

1 ounce Cherry Heering

1 ounce sweet vermouth

Glass: coupe

Garnish: amarena cherry

Fill a coupe with ice to chill. In an ice-filled
shaker, add all of the ingredients and shake
for about 15 seconds. Empty ice from coupe
and strain cocktail into it. Garnish with
amarena cherry.

Sazerac

A Sazerac isn't a Sazerac without Peychaud's bitters. In the 1830s, Antoine Peychaud, the owner of a New Orleans apothecary, began dispensing his proprietary, high-proof tonic, which was infused with numerous herbs and botanicals. This early cure-all was deep red in color, with complex cherry and anise notes—especially tasty for a patent medicine. The formula was soon requested at other establishments around New Orleans. By 1850, the Sazerac Coffee House on Royal Street was serving Peychaud's bitters mixed with its Sazerac de Forge et Fils Cognac, a product that it imported exclusively from France. The concoction became known as a Sazerac.

PEYCHAUD'S

AROMATIC COCKTAIL BITTERS

DIPLOMA OF HONOR
AWARDED AT
THE GRAND EXHIBITION OF ALTONA-GERMANY, 1869

RYE

COGNAC

ABSINTHE

SCENE IN NEW ORLEANS.

New Orleans is built on a bend of the Mississippi in the form of a crescent (that is, the form of the new moon), and on that account is sometimes called the "Crescent City."

When France's phylloxera epidemic in the 1880s dried up imports of Cognac, the Sazerac Coffee House, and others, switched to rye whiskey in their Sazeracs.

Should you order a Sazerac today—best pursued at a dimly-lit, classic haunt like Tujague's or the Napoleon House, both in the French Quarter—a rye-based cocktail is what you'll be served. But beyond the base, there are dozens of variations to the formula. Some call for Angostura bitters, or a mix of Angostura and Peychaud's. But there's no denying the bright affinity Peychaud's bitters has for the absinthe in this recipe—use Peychaud's only for a match greater than the sum of its parts.

SAZERAC

¼ ounce absinthe, for rinse

1 sugar cube

3 to 5 dashes Peychaud's bitters

2 ounces rye whiskey or Cognac

Glass: rocks glass

Garnish: wide strip of lemon rind

Pour absinthe into a rocks glass and roll the liquid around the inside of the glass. Pour out any remaining absinthe, so you're left with an absinthe-rinsed glass. In a separate rocks glass, add the sugar cube and Peychaud's bitters; muddle. Add whiskey or Cognac and stir. Pour concoction back into the absinthe-rinsed glass, and add a large ice cube or several medium-sized cubes. Squeeze the lemon rind over the cocktail to release its oil, and submerge the rind into the cocktail.

southern section of our country, and is the most important cotton market in the world.

New Orleans

It is the largest city in all the

Manhattan

A Manhattan cocktail conveys the uptown style of Madison Avenue advertising executives before Prohibition, sipping their drinks at swanky hotel bars like the Hoffman House, where the grand saloon featured seventeen white-vested bartenders per shift, a massive wood-carved bar, and Bouguereau's twelve-foot-high mural of *Nymphs and Satyr*. The orgy-depicting painting is much like the Manhattan cocktail itself: elegant and tasteful, yet indulgent and a little naughty. The 1923 *Valentine's Manual of Old New York* contains an article written by a bartender who worked at New York's Hoffman House in the 1880s. He wrote that the Manhattan was invented in the 1860s "by a man named Black" who kept a bar south of Houston Street.

NATURAL WHISKEY MATURED IN WOOD.

VERMOUTH

Manhattan

The first printed reference of the Manhattan cocktail occurs in a New York newspaper in 1882, noting, "It is but a short time ago that a mixture of whiskey, vermouth and bitters came into vogue."

While early recipes were made with rye whiskey, bourbon has become the Manhattan base of choice in recent years. Rye gives a spicy kick, while bourbon makes a sweeter cocktail. But with regard to its supporting ingredients, the Manhattan has dried out over the years. Where early recipes called for equal parts of sweet vermouth and whiskey, today's versions now recommend two or three parts whiskey to one part vermouth. Feel free to experiment—we won't tell.

MANHATTAN

2 ounces rye whiskey (or bourbon)

1 ounce sweet vermouth

3 dashes Angostura bitters

Glass: martini

Garnish: amarena cherry

Fill a martini glass with ice to chill. In an ice-filled mixing glass, add all of the ingredients and mix for about 15 seconds. Empty ice from glass and strain cocktail into it. Drop amarena cherry into the cocktail to garnish.

PERFECT MANHATTAN
A "perfect" cocktail features dry and sweet vermouth, like this subtle twist on a Manhattan that some connoisseurs prefer. To the classic formula, reduce sweet vermouth to half an ounce, and add half an ounce of dry vermouth as well.

Wassail

"Here we come a-wassailing / Among the leaves so green, Here we come a-wand'ring / So fair to be seen." So goes the first verse of "The Wassail Song," an English Christmas song that evokes young carolers serenading their neighbors, spreading good cheer.

The tradition of wassailing is thought to extend all the way back to the twelfth century—wassail comes from the Middle English *waes haeil,* to toast one's health. In those pagan times, farmers prayed to Pomona, the goddess of fruit trees, to bless the next year's crop. Into the early twentieth century, English farmers and their crews would take a wassail bowl into the orchard to salute the apple trees with a blessing.

The wassail ceremony required the farmer and his workers to circle around the tree and sing songs, repeatedly strike the tree's trunk, place toasted bread on its branches, and, finally, to shoot into the tree with a gun, actions that were meant to persuade the tree (and its attendant spirits) into producing a better crop the following season.

The wassail bowl's ingredients were as eclectic (by today's standards) as the ceremony. Hundreds of recipes exist, based variously on wine, beer, or cider, along with ingredients like eggs and toast. These days, wassail bowls are more likely to skip some of the more unusual ingredients, resulting in a generously spiked hot cider. While the recipe requires a bit of effort, it pays off in a hot, festive holiday punch that makes any kitchen smell like Christmas.

WASSAIL

20 whole cloves

5 small cooking apples

2 quarts hard apple cider (or red wine)

4 cinnamon sticks

10 allspice berries

½ teaspoon nutmeg, grated

1 orange

2 cups cup Cognac, Calvados, or brandy

Glass: punch cup or glass mug

Preheat oven to 375°F. Stick cloves into apples, and bake in oven for 45 minutes. Fill Dutch oven with apple cider and remaining spices. Simmer over medium heat. Add cooked apples and simmer for a few hours. When ready to serve, add brandy and orange rinds, and allow to heat for a few minutes, then serve hot in punch cups.

Acknowledgements

From the Author

I'd like to raise a glass to toast (and thank) several people. First and foremost, this book would not have been possible without the vision and support of the ace publishing team at Random House, including publisher Amanda D'Acierno, creative director Fabrizio La Rocca, editor Maren Monitello, designers Chie Ushio and Tina Malaney, publicists Katie Fleming and Alex Chernin, and many others.

Poul Lange brought these stories to life with his phenomenal illustrations. Kayoko Suzuki-Lange also played a crucial role as stylist (and chief garnish artist) on our photo shoots.

Greg Boehm, owner of Cocktail Kingdom and publisher of Puddle Jumper Books generously allowed me access to his vast collection of historic cocktail books. The glassware companies Riedel and Nachtmann provided glasses for our photo shoots. Campari, Louis Royer Cognac, Santa Teresa Rum, Hennessy, and Mandarine Napoléon were among the spirits companies that provided product support. Developer Iain Lawson helped bring StoriedSips.com to fruition. Hanna Lee (and her team at Hanna Lee Communications) generously assisted with publicity efforts.

I'd also like to thank cocktail historians like David Wondrich and William Grimes whose deeply researched works have set the bar for cocktail writing.

I am indebted to my husband, Jono Pandolfi and daughter Gia Pandolfi, for their patience as I spent nights and weekends writing (and tasting!) my way through this project. Finally, I would like to thank both of our families for their unconditional support.

From the Illustrator

I want to thank Erica Duecy for coming up with the concept for this book, executing it so beautifully, and allowing me to be part of it. Not only did I have fun making these collages, I also learned a lot about the history of mixology, and got to taste all the 40 cocktails during the photo shoots*.

I'd like to join Erica in her appreciation of the Random House team, who made the whole process so smooth and enjoyable. And thanks to my old pal from SVA, Fabrizio La Rocca, for thinking of me for the project.

My wife has been incredibly tolerant of my paper scraps and glue tracks around the house, but more than that, her keen sense of style and ways with a fruit slicer became essential to the photo shoots. Thank you, Kayoko.

The golden age of cocktails overlaps some highly creative periods in the world of graphic design. In my collages for this book I relied heavily on the beautiful label and advertisement designs of those bygone days. I'd like to express my great appreciation for the numerous and nameless designers who created this material.

And finally I would like to thank Ernest Hemingway for adding grapefruit juice to his Daiquiri while finding time to write all those books.

*A special thank you to Nikon for their reliable auto-focus system.

ABOUT THE AUTHOR

Erica Duecy is an award-winning writer and editor specializing in Wine & Spirits and Travel. By day, she runs the Fodor's Travel website as Deputy Editor. At night, Erica tastes wines and tests cocktail recipes for her blog, storiedsips.com, and the luxury alpine travel magazine *SNOW* (Bonnier Publishing), where she was Wine & Spirits Editor for the past six years. For *SNOW*, Erica has written wine and spirit features ranging from the new generation of Wild West whiskeys to extreme winemaking and skiing in New Zealand, as well documenting hot après-ski cocktail trends around the globe.

She is a long-time judge for the James Beard Journalism Awards, and holds an Advanced Certificate, with distinction, from the London-based Wine & Spirits Education Trust (WSET). For her wine and spirits writing, Duecy was awarded the 2010 Peju Fellowship by the Symposium for Professional Wine Writers. She has written for the the *New York Times*, *Food & Wine*, and numerous other publications.

ABOUT THE ILLUSTRATOR

Poul Lange is a Danish designer, illustrator, and photographer. He lived and worked in New York for over 20 years before relocating to Los Angeles in 2013. In Europe he is best known for his book jacket designs for writers such as Siri Hustvedt, Paul Auster, Charles Bukowski, Ernest Hemingway, and Anne Rice. His collage-based illustrations have been printed in the *New York Times*, *Boston Globe*, *GQ Magazine*, *Time Magazine*, et al.

His collages have been shown in galleries in Copenhagen, New York, Nashville and Los Angeles.

Lange's children's book *The Book of Holes* (2006), which he wrote and illustrated was published in Denmark and was chosen as one of the year's 50 best designed books by American Institute of Graphic Arts, one of many awards his work has won. *The Book of Holes* is now available as an iPad app from Chocolate Factory Publications.

Bibliography

Alvey, R. Gerald. *Kentucky Bluegrass Country*. University
    Press of Mississippi. 1992.

Amenomori, N. *The Grand Hotel, Limited, Guide Book for
    Yokohama and Immediate Vicinity*. 1898. Accessed
    October 2012: http://www.baxleystamps.com/litho/
    meiji/grand_guide_c1898.shtml

Aperol. Palm Bay International Fine Wine & Spirits.
    Accessed September 2012: http://www.palmbay.com/
    aperol-aperol.htm

"Aperol Fact Sheet." Palm Bay International Fine Wine &
    Spirits. Accessed September 2012: http://www.palmbay.
    com/databaseimages/technicalsheets/Aperol_TS.pdf

Aperol website. Italy. Accessed September 2012: http://www.
    aperol.it/

Arnold, Eric. "What the World Drinks." Forbes.com.
    December 23, 2008. Accessed December 2012: http://

www.forbes.com/2008/12/23/vodka-scotch-spirits-forbeslife-cx_ea_1223spirits.html

"Art: Tales of the Hoffman House," *Time Magazine*. Monday, Jan. 25, 1943.

Atkins, Susy. "Wine Review: Kir Royale." *The Telegraph*. London: August 6, 2012. Accessed October 2012: http://www.telegraph.co.uk/foodanddrink/wine/9442212/Wine-Review-Kir-Royale.html

Baker, Charles H., Jr. *The Gentleman's Companion, Vol. II.*, Derrydale Press, 1939.

Beebe, Lucius. *The Stork Club Bar Book*. Rinehart and Co., New York, 1946. Reprint: New Day Publishing, 2003.

Bergeron, Victor "Trader Vic." *Trader Vic's Book of Food and Drink*, 1946. Reprint: Random House Value Pub, 1982.

Bianchi, Francesca Cesa. "Harry's Bar of Venice—a modern Italian landmark." CNN.com, October 13, 2000. Accessed November 2012: http://archives.cnn.com/2000/FOOD/news/10/13/harrys.bar/

Brown, Henry Collins, ed. *Valentine's Manual of Old New York*. Vol 7. 1923.

Brown, Jared McDaniel and Anistatia Renard Miller, et al. *Cuba: The Legend of Rum*. Havana Club International, 2009.

Burke, David. *Writers in Paris: Literary Lives in the City of Light*. Counterpoint Press, Mar 23, 2010.

Caffe Giacosa website. Accessed November 2012: http://www.caffegiacosa.it/index.php?file=history

"Canon Kir Dies at 92." *Catholic Herald*. London: May 3, 1968. Accessed October 2012: http://archive.catholicherald.co.uk/article/3rd-may-1968/2/canon-kir-dies-at-92

Coldicott, Nicholas. "Bamboo: Japan's sherry amour." *The Japan Times*. June 26, 2009. Accessed October 2012: http://info.japantimes.co.jp/text/fg20090626nc.html

Coulombe, Charles A. *The Muse in the Bottle: Great Writers on the Joy of Drinking*. Citadel Press, 2002.

Coulombe, Charles A. *Rum: The Epic Story of the Drink that Changed the World*. Citadel Press, 2005.

Craddock, Harry. *The Savoy Cocktail Book*. (1930). Reprint: Pavilion, 2007.

Crockett, Albert S. *The Old Waldorf-Astoria Bar Book* (Classic Cocktail Books series). Reprint 2003.

Curtis, Wayne. "The Old Man and the Daiquiri."
The Atlantic. October 2005.

Danker, Leslie. Phone interview. October 24, 2012.

DeGroff, Dale. *Craft of the Cocktail*, Clarkson Potter, New
York: October 15, 2002.

De Kuyper, Marc. Phone interview, October 26, 2012.

"The Democracy in Trouble." *Chicago Daily Tribune*,
February 15, 1880.

The Detroit Athletic Club website. Accessed October 2012:
http://www.thedac.com/public/news/ePreview/2009/
_issue0921/rooms_slideshow.html

Difford, Simon. "Bellini." *Diffords Guide to Cocktails: v. 7*.
Sauce Guides Limited, London: February 15, 2008.

Ellwood, Mark. "The Sipping Point," *New York Times*.
March 13, 2005.

Ensslin, Hugo R. "New foreword (by David Wondrich)."
Recipes for Mixed Drinks. Reprint: Mud Puddle Books
Inc., 2009.

Felten, Eric. "Maybe Mamie, Maybe Not." *Wall Street
Journal*. July 19, 2008.

Field, Colin Peter. *The Cocktails of the Ritz Paris*. Simon & Schuster, London: May 6, 2003.

"Gin Fizz." Libertine Parfumerie. Accessed October 2012: http://www.libertineparfumerie.com.au/gin-fizz/w1/ i1001858/

Goslings Rum website. Accessed December 2012: http://www.goslingsrum.com/discover_ourhistory.asp

The Grand Hotel, Limited (advertisement). *Cocktails 101*. September 2011. Accessed October 2012: http://cocktail101.files.wordpress.com/2011/09/grand-hotel-yokohama-ad.jpg

Grieve, M. "Gentians." Botanical.com. Accessed September 2012: http://botanical.com/botanical/mgmh/g/gentia08.html

Grimes, William. *Straight Up or On the Rocks*. North Point Press, Berkeley, California: 2001.

Harrison, Karen Tina. "Jersey Lightning." *New Jersey Monthly*. July 13, 2009. Accessed October 2012: http://njmonthly.com/articles/restaurants/jersey-lightning.html

Harry's Bar in Venice website. Accessed November 2012: http://www.harrysbarvenezia.com/

Hasler, P.W., ed. *The History of Parliament: the House of Commons 1558-1603*. Tso, London: 1981.

"Have You Seen Tom Collins?" *The Elk County Advocate*. Ridgeway, Pa: May 28, 1874. Accessed November 2012: http://chroniclingamerica.loc.gov/lccn/ sn84026259/1874-05-28/ed-1/seq-4/

Hazlitt, W. Carew. *The Popular Antiquities of Great Britain: Faith and Folklore*, Reeves and Turner, London: 1905

Hotchner, A.E. "A Legend as Big as the Ritz." *Vanity Fair*. July 2012.

"Kir Royale." Diffordsguide.com. London. Accessed October 2012: http://www.diffordsguide.com/cocktails/ recipe/1109/kir-royale

Merrill, Dennis. *Negotiating Paradise: U.S. Tourism and Empire in Twentieth-Century Latin America*. University of North Carolina Press, 2009.

Moruzzi, Peter. *Havana Before Castro: When Cuba Was a Tropical Playground*. Gibbs Smith, 2008.

"The most legendary bar in Paris turns 100," *Sydney Morning Herald*. Nov. 24, 2011. http://www.smh.com.au/travel/ travel-news/the-most-legendary-bar-in-paris-turns-100- 20111124-1nvw9.html

Newman, Kara. "The Spirited Traveller: Having the last word in Detroit." Reuters. November 8, 2011. Accessed October 2012: http://www.reuters.com/ article/2011/11/08/us-spirited-traveller-detroit- idUSTRE7A74J320111108

Nickell, Joe. *The Kentucky Mint Julep*. University Press of
Kentucky, 2003.

"Once Upon a Time in Mexico," *Imbibe* Magazine. March/
April 2010. Accessed October 2012: http://imbibe.com/
feature/once-upon-time-in-mexico/7589

Parsons, Brad Thomas. *Bitters: A Spirited History of a Classic
Cure-All, with Cocktails, Recipes, and Formulas*. Random
House, New York: 2011.

"Planter's Punch! A West Indian Recipe," *Fun*, vol 27-28.
London: September 4, 1878.

Untitled article. *The Post Standard*. Syracuse, New York.
March 7, 1902.

Regan, Gary and Mardee Haidin Regan. "The Birth of
the Cosmopolitan: A Tale of Two Bartenders, Ardent
Spirits newsletter, Vol. 7, 2007. Accessed October 2012:
http://web.archive.org/web/20071028165129/http://
www.ardentspirits.com/ardentspirits/Newsletter/
vol7Issue06.html

Regan, Gary. "The Cocktailian: Negroni history lesson
ends in a glass." *SFGate.com*. March 29, 2009. Accessed
November 2012. http://www.sfgate.com/recipes/article/
The-Cocktailian-Negroni-history-lesson-ends-
in-a-3246697.php

Regan, Gary. *The Joy of Mixology: The Consummate Guide to the Bartender's Craft*. Clarkson Potter, New York: 2003.

Rothbaum, Noah. *The Business of Spirits: How Savvy Marketers, Innovative Distillers, and Entrepreneurs Changed How We Drink*. Kaplan Publishing, 2007.

"Rum! Rum! Rum!" *The Balance and Columbian Repository*. Vol. V, No. 18. May 6, 1806. Hudson, New York. Accessed November 2012: http://www.museumoftheamericancocktail.org/museum/TheBalance.html

Russell, Sir Herbert. *With the Prince in the East; a record of the royal visit to India and Japan*. Methuen & Co., London: 1922.

Sampson, Susan. "A Caribbean Tale of Two Piña Coladas," *Toronto Star*, Dec. 29, 2004.

Sazerac website. Accessed December 2012: http://www.sazerac.com/cocktail.aspx

Sterling and Kroch, Carl, eds. *So Red the Nose, or Breath in the Afternoon*, Farrar Rinehart, 1935.

The Stork Club website. Accessed November 2012: http://www.stork-club.com/celebrities-at-the-stork-club.html

Sullivan, Ed. "Hollywood." *The Pittsburgh Press*. September 20, 1939.

Untitled article. *The Sunday herald and weekly national intelligencer*, Washington D.C., August 3, 1890. Accessed December 2012: http://chroniclingamerica.loc.gov/lccn/sn82016373/1890-08-03/ed-1/seq-4/

Sutcliffe, Theodora. "Bar Icons—Fosco Scarselli." *Class Magazine*. May 23, 2011. Accessed November 2012: http://www.diffordsguide.com/class-magazine/read-online/en/2011-05-24/page-9/bar-icons

Sutcliffe, Theodora. "Harry Craddock." *Class Magazine*. January 10, 2012. Accessed October 2012: http://www.diffordsguide.com/class-magazine/read-online/en/2012-01-10/page-4/bar-icon

Thomas, Jerry. *How to Mix Drinks, or the Bon Vivant's Companion*. Dick & Fitzgerald, New York: 1862.

Thompson, Fred. *Bourbon: 50 Rousing Recipes for a Classic American Spirit*. Houghton Mifflin Harcourt, 2010.

Thring, Oliver. "Consider Pimms." *The Guardian*, United Kingdom. May 18, 2010.

"To the Editor of the Balance." *The Balance and Columbian Repository*. Vol. V, No. 19. May 13, 1806. Hudson, New York. Accessed November 2012: http://www.museumoftheamericancocktail.org/museum/TheBalance.html

"Tom Collins is my Name." Music Copyright Deposits, 1870-1885. (Microfilm M 3500) Songs with piano.

Accessed November 2012: http://lcweb2.loc.gov/diglib/ihas/loc.music.sm1874.09822

Tooley, Sarah A. "Old Christmas Customs in the Counties," *The English Illustrated Magazine*, *Vol. 30*. Hutchinson and Company, London: 1904.

"Valentino Loses Battle with Death." The Plattsville Sentinel. Plattsville, New York. August 24, 1926.

Vanderwood, Paul J. *Satan's Playground: Mobsters and Movie Stars at America's Greatest Gaming Resort*. Duke University Press, 2010.

"Wassailing!" The Hymns and Carols of Christmas website. Accessed December 2012: http://www.hymnsandcarolsofchristmas.com/Hymns_and_Carols/Notes_On_Carols/wassailing.htm

Weir, Joanne. *Tequila*. Ten Speed Press, New York: 2009.

Whitford, David. "Gosling's Rum: Promoting the spirit of Bermuda." CNNMoney.com. April 15, 2011. Accessed Debember 2012: http://management.fortune.cnn.com/2011/04/15/goslings-rum-promoting-the-spirit-of-bermuda/

Wickware, Francis Sill. "Liquor: Famous American Bars." *LIFE Magazine*. May 27, 1946.

Wondrich, David. "How the Sling Was Slung." *Imbibe Magazine*. July/August 2011.

Wondrich, David. *Imbibe!: From Absinthe Cocktail to Whiskey Smash, a Salute in Stories and Drinks to "Professor" Jerry Thomas, Pioneer of the American Bar*. Perigee Trade, 2007.

Wondrich, David. "Mimosa." *Esquire.com*. New York. Accessed October 2012: http://www.esquire.com/drinks/mimosa-drink-recipe